Glorifying Grace Prayer Journal
By Imani M-Glover
Copyright© 2018 by Imani M-Glover
Published by Imani M-Glover
Under Sophisticated Press LLC

PRINTED IN THE UNITED STATES OF AMERICA

Book Design by Sophisticated Press LLC
ISBN 978-0-9988669-8-7

Scriptures marked NIV are taken from the NEW INTERNATIONAL VERSION (NIV): Scripture taken from THE HOLY BIBLE, NEW INTERNATIONAL VERSION ®. Copyright© 1973, 1978, 1984, 2011 by Biblica, Inc.™. Used by permission of Zondervan

SOPHISTICATED
PRESS

Acknowledgements

Special thanks to the following people that supported this project. The Holy Spirit, my Husband Cedric G., my late Mother Lucy, my son Solomon G., my son Kwame' G., my grandmother Rosa Lee , Work Bible Studies w/ Valarie Mathews, my Aunt Ernestine, Acts Full Gospel Church, Declare Victory prayer call (Dionne Jackson), San Diego Bible Study w/ Pastor Edith, Marriage Matters prayer call, Sophisticated Press LLC, Wives Who War sisters, Dawn King, LaSonda McDuffie and Cassandra Weatherby. I would also like to thank Mahogany Pages Book club (edt. 2001) and California Suga Book Club. Barbara Marshall. To all of my family and close friends, thank you for your support whether you have taken my phone calls, listen to me vent, supported me, encouraged me, prayed with me or for me, and most importantly loved up on me.

Imani M-Glover

Foreword

When Imani asked me to pen the foreword for her journal I was honored. I felt compelled to do so. I had just come off an emotional roller coaster where journaling had a very healing effect on my life after dedicating nearly 20 years of my life working as a public servant, where I gave of myself daily. I was responsible for ensuring that juveniles were in compliance with their court orders, they attended school as directed, maintained appropriate behavior in the community and at home, and ultimately monitored their behavior to ensure that they did not have any new law violations. As part of my job, I was also an advocate for the juveniles at school to ensure that they were being treated fairly and that their rights were not violated due to their probation status. I was responsible for writing court recommendations for appropriate services and sanctions for new laws and probation violations.

With staffing at my place of employment being at an all-time low, this meant inheriting additional workloads and responsibilities. After about two years, my job broke me down to the point where I felt compassion fatigue. I felt that the job had siphoned all of my energy and emotions. I had nothing left to give. One morning while in my supervisor's office discussing my caseload, I began to feel a tightening in my left arm and leg. As a result, I was rushed to the emergency department from my place of employment. I was literally on the brink of a stroke. I was taken off of work for a month and given a prescription for blood pressure medication. My reflections began immediately. I started by asking myself, "how did I allow myself to get to this place?" I was committed to finding holistic healing for myself.

I reached out to Imani for support and advice on how to heal myself and get off of the emotional roller coaster. Imani prayed with me, she provided me with several scriptures one of them was Psalms 91:1, and she suggested that I journal my feelings.

I began to journal throughout the day, writing down my thoughts, prayers, feelings, fears, my stumbling blocks, my goals, and my triumphs. This process has been so therapeutic and allowed me to be introspective in a way that I had not been in a very long time. My focus selfishly shifted from others and I began to focus on me. Because of journaling I am healing daily. What I have come to know with all certainty is the power of journaling. You can pray and journal things into existence.

I am excited for this wonderful woman who I consider to be a friend. Here she is again, looking at ways to pour into the lives of others. Imani I already see you healing the world one journal at a time. I know this will effect positive change.

Much Respect,

LaShonda McDuffie

2019 Calendar

January

S	M	T	W	T	F	S
		1	2	3	4	5
6	7	8	9	10	11	12
13	14	15	16	17	18	19
20	21	22	23	24	25	26
27	28	29	30	31		

February

S	M	T	W	T	F	S
					1	2
3	4	5	6	7	8	9
10	11	12	13	14	15	16
17	18	19	20	21	22	23
24	25	26	27	28		

March

S	M	T	W	T	F	S
					1	2
3	4	5	6	7	8	9
10	11	12	13	14	15	16
17	18	19	20	21	22	23
24	25	26	27	28	29	30
31						

April

S	M	T	W	T	F	S
	1	2	3	4	5	6
7	8	9	10	11	12	13
14	15	16	17	18	19	20
21	22	23	24	25	26	27
28	29	30				

May

S	M	T	W	T	F	S
			1	2	3	4
5	6	7	8	9	10	11
12	13	14	15	16	17	18
19	20	21	22	23	24	25
26	27	28	29	30	31	

June

S	M	T	W	T	F	S
						1
2	3	4	5	6	7	8
9	10	11	12	13	14	15
16	17	18	19	20	21	22
23	24	25	26	27	28	29
30						

July

S	M	T	W	T	F	S
	1	2	3	4	5	6
7	8	9	10	11	12	13
14	15	16	17	18	19	20
21	22	23	24	25	26	27
28	29	30	31			

August

S	M	T	W	T	F	S
				1	2	3
4	5	6	7	8	9	10
11	12	13	14	15	16	17
18	19	20	21	22	23	24
25	26	27	28	29	30	31

September

S	M	T	W	T	F	S
1	2	3	4	5	6	7
8	9	10	11	12	13	14
15	16	17	18	19	20	21
22	23	24	25	26	27	28
29	30					

October

S	M	T	W	T	F	S
		1	2	3	4	5
6	7	8	9	10	11	12
13	14	15	16	17	18	19
20	21	22	23	24	25	26
27	28	29	30	31		

November

S	M	T	W	T	F	S
					1	2
3	4	5	6	7	8	9
10	11	12	13	14	15	16
17	18	19	20	21	22	23
24	25	26	27	28	29	30

December

S	M	T	W	T	F	S
1	2	3	4	5	6	7
8	9	10	11	12	13	14
15	16	17	18	19	20	21
22	23	24	25	26	27	28
29	30	31				

Important Dates

1   January 🦋🦋🦋🦋🦋 New Year's Day
21 January 🦋🦋🦋🦋🦋 MLK Birthday
14 February 🦋🦋🦋🦋🦋 Valentine Day
18 February 🦋🦋🦋🦋🦋 President's Day
21 April   🦋🦋🦋🦋🦋🦋 Easter Day
12 May   🦋🦋🦋🦋🦋🦋 Mother's Day
27 May   🦋🦋🦋🦋🦋🦋 Memorial Day
16 June   🦋🦋🦋🦋🦋🦋 Father's Day
4   July   🦋🦋🦋🦋🦋🦋🦋 Independence Day
2   September 🦋🦋🦋🦋🦋 Labor Day
11 November 🦋🦋🦋🦋🦋 Veteran's Day
28 November 🦋🦋🦋🦋🦋 Thanksgiving Day
24 December 🦋🦋🦋🦋🦋 Christmas Eve
25 December 🦋🦋🦋🦋🦋 Christmas Day

Let Us Pray

Prayer Journal

TITLE: _____ DATE: _____ / _____ / _____

RELEVANT SCRIPTURES:

1. _____ 2. _____ 3. _____
4. _____ 5. _____ 6. _____

CONTENT OF PRAYER REQUEST

_____
_____
_____
_____

THE LORDS ANSWER WAS: DATE: _____ / _____ / _____
YES
NO
NOT YET

HOW THE LORD ANSWERED MY PRAYER

_____
_____
_____
_____

DETAIL OF DELIVERY / LESSON LEARNED

_____
_____
_____
_____

SIGNATURE OF ACCOUNTABILITY _____

PSALM 91:1 WHOEVER DWELLS IN THE SHELTER OF THE MOST HIGH
WILL REST IN THE SHADOW OF THE ALMIGHTY.

Prayer Journal

TITLE: _____   DATE: _____ / _____ / _____

RELEVANT SCRIPTURES:

1. _____ 2. _____ 3. _____
4. _____ 5. _____ 6. _____

CONTENT OF PRAYER REQUEST

_____
_____
_____
_____

THE LORDS ANSWER WAS: DATE: _____ / _____ / _____
YES
NO
NOT YET

HOW THE LORD ANSWERED MY PRAYER

_____
_____
_____
_____

DETAIL OF DELIVERY / LESSON LEARNED

_____
_____
_____
_____

SIGNATURE OF ACCOUNTABILITY _____

Prayer Journal

TITLE: _____ DATE: _____ / _____ / _____

RELEVANT SCRIPTURES:

1. _____ 2. _____ 3. _____
4. _____ 5. _____ 6. _____

CONTENT OF PRAYER REQUEST

_____
_____
_____
_____

THE LORDS ANSWER WAS: DATE: _____ / _____ / _____
YES
NO
NOT YET

HOW THE LORD ANSWERED MY PRAYER

_____
_____
_____
_____

DETAIL OF DELIVERY / LESSON LEARNED

_____
_____
_____
_____

SIGNATURE OF ACCOUNTABILITY _____

PSALM 91:2 I WILL SAY OF THE LORD, "HE IS MY REFUGE AND MY FORTRESS, MY GOD, IN WHOM I TRUST."

Prayer Journal

TITLE: _____   DATE: _____ / _____ / _____

RELEVANT SCRIPTURES:

1. _____ 2. _____ 3. _____
4. _____ 5. _____ 6. _____

CONTENT OF PRAYER REQUEST

_____
_____
_____
_____

THE LORDS ANSWER WAS: DATE: _____ / _____ / _____
YES
NO
NOT YET

HOW THE LORD ANSWERED MY PRAYER

_____
_____
_____
_____

DETAIL OF DELIVERY / LESSON LEARNED

_____
_____
_____
_____

SIGNATURE OF ACCOUNTABILITY _____

Prayer Journal

TITLE: _____   DATE: _____ / _____ / _____

RELEVANT SCRIPTURES:
1. _____ 2. _____ 3. _____
4. _____ 5. _____ 6. _____

CONTENT OF PRAYER REQUEST

_____
_____
_____
_____

THE LORDS ANSWER WAS: DATE: _____ / _____ / _____
YES
NO
NOT YET

HOW THE LORD ANSWERED MY PRAYER

_____
_____
_____
_____

DETAIL OF DELIVERY / LESSON LEARNED

_____
_____
_____
_____

SIGNATURE OF ACCOUNTABILITY _____

PSALM 91:3 SURELY HE WILL SAVE YOU FROM THE FOWLER'S SNARE
AND FROM THE DEADLY PESTILENCE.

Prayer Journal

TITLE: _____   DATE: _____ / _____ / _____

RELEVANT SCRIPTURES:

1. _____ 2. _____ 3. _____
4. _____ 5. _____ 6. _____

CONTENT OF PRAYER REQUEST

_____
_____
_____
_____

THE LORDS ANSWER WAS: DATE: _____ / _____ / _____
YES
NO
NOT YET

HOW THE LORD ANSWERED MY PRAYER

_____
_____
_____
_____

DETAIL OF DELIVERY / LESSON LEARNED

_____
_____
_____
_____

SIGNATURE OF ACCOUNTABILITY _____

Prayer Journal

TITLE: _____ DATE: _____ / _____ / _____

RELEVANT SCRIPTURES:

1. _____ 2. _____ 3. _____
4. _____ 5. _____ 6. _____

CONTENT OF PRAYER REQUEST

_____
_____
_____
_____

THE LORDS ANSWER WAS: DATE: _____ / _____ / _____
YES
NO
NOT YET

HOW THE LORD ANSWERED MY PRAYER

_____
_____
_____
_____

DETAIL OF DELIVERY / LESSON LEARNED

_____
_____
_____
_____

SIGNATURE OF ACCOUNTABILITY _____

PSALM 91:4 HE WILL COVER YOU WITH HIS FEATHERS, AND UNDER HIS WINGS YOU WILL FIND REFUGE; HIS FAITHFULNESS WILL BE YOUR SHIELD AND RAMPART.

Prayer Journal

TITLE: _____ DATE: _____ / _____ / _____

RELEVANT SCRIPTURES:

1. _____ 2. _____ 3. _____
4. _____ 5. _____ 6. _____

CONTENT OF PRAYER REQUEST

_____
_____
_____
_____

THE LORDS ANSWER WAS: DATE: _____ / _____ / _____
YES
NO
NOT YET

HOW THE LORD ANSWERED MY PRAYER

_____
_____
_____
_____

DETAIL OF DELIVERY / LESSON LEARNED

_____
_____
_____
_____

SIGNATURE OF ACCOUNTABILITY _____

Prayer Journal

TITLE: _____   DATE: _____ / _____ / _____

RELEVANT SCRIPTURES:

1. _____ 2. _____ 3. _____
4. _____ 5. _____ 6. _____

CONTENT OF PRAYER REQUEST

_____
_____
_____
_____

THE LORDS ANSWER WAS: DATE: _____ / _____ / _____
YES
NO
NOT YET

HOW THE LORD ANSWERED MY PRAYER

_____
_____
_____
_____

DETAIL OF DELIVERY / LESSON LEARNED

_____
_____
_____
_____

SIGNATURE OF ACCOUNTABILITY _____

PSALM 91:5 YOU WILL NOT FEAR THE TERROR OF NIGHT,
NOR THE ARROW THAT FLIES BY DAY

Prayer Journal

TITLE: _____   DATE: _____ / _____ / _____

RELEVANT SCRIPTURES:

1. _____ 2. _____ 3. _____
4. _____ 5. _____ 6. _____

CONTENT OF PRAYER REQUEST

_____
_____
_____
_____

THE LORDS ANSWER WAS: DATE: _____ / _____ / _____
YES
NO
NOT YET

HOW THE LORD ANSWERED MY PRAYER

_____
_____
_____
_____

DETAIL OF DELIVERY / LESSON LEARNED

_____
_____
_____
_____

SIGNATURE OF ACCOUNTABILITY _____

Prayer Journal

TITLE: _____ DATE: _____ / _____ / _____

RELEVANT SCRIPTURES:

1. _____ 2. _____ 3. _____
4. _____ 5. _____ 6. _____

CONTENT OF PRAYER REQUEST

_____
_____
_____
_____

THE LORDS ANSWER WAS: DATE: _____ / _____ / _____
YES
NO
NOT YET

HOW THE LORD ANSWERED MY PRAYER

_____
_____
_____
_____

DETAIL OF DELIVERY / LESSON LEARNED

_____
_____
_____
_____

SIGNATURE OF ACCOUNTABILITY _____

PSALM 91:6 NOR THE PESTILENCE THAT STALKS IN THE DARKNESS,
NOR THE PLAGUE THAT DESTROYS AT MIDDAY.

Prayer Journal

TITLE: _____ DATE: _____ / _____ / _____

RELEVANT SCRIPTURES:

1. _____ 2. _____ 3. _____
4. _____ 5. _____ 6. _____

CONTENT OF PRAYER REQUEST

_____
_____
_____
_____

THE LORDS ANSWER WAS: DATE: _____ / _____ / _____
YES
NO
NOT YET

HOW THE LORD ANSWERED MY PRAYER

_____
_____
_____
_____

DETAIL OF DELIVERY / LESSON LEARNED

_____
_____
_____
_____

SIGNATURE OF ACCOUNTABILITY _____

Prayer Journal

TITLE: _____ DATE: _____ / _____ / _____

RELEVANT SCRIPTURES:

1. _____ 2. _____ 3. _____
4. _____ 5. _____ 6. _____

CONTENT OF PRAYER REQUEST

_____
_____
_____
_____

THE LORDS ANSWER WAS: DATE: _____ / _____ / _____
YES
NO
NOT YET

HOW THE LORD ANSWERED MY PRAYER

_____
_____
_____
_____

DETAIL OF DELIVERY / LESSON LEARNED

_____
_____
_____
_____

SIGNATURE OF ACCOUNTABILITY _____

PSALM 91:7 A THOUSAND MAY FALL AT YOUR SIDE, TEN THOUSAND AT YOUR RIGHT HAND, BUT IT WILL NOT COME NEAR YOU.

Prayer Journal

TITLE: _____   DATE: _____ / _____ / _____

RELEVANT SCRIPTURES:

1. _____ 2. _____ 3. _____
4. _____ 5. _____ 6. _____

CONTENT OF PRAYER REQUEST

_____
_____
_____
_____

THE LORDS ANSWER WAS: DATE: _____ / _____ / _____
YES
NO
NOT YET

HOW THE LORD ANSWERED MY PRAYER

_____
_____
_____
_____

DETAIL OF DELIVERY / LESSON LEARNED

_____
_____
_____
_____

SIGNATURE OF ACCOUNTABILITY _____

Prayer Journal

TITLE: _____   DATE: _____ / _____ / _____

RELEVANT SCRIPTURES:

1. _____ 2. _____ 3. _____
4. _____ 5. _____ 6. _____

CONTENT OF PRAYER REQUEST

_____
_____
_____
_____

THE LORDS ANSWER WAS: DATE: _____ / _____ / _____
YES
NO
NOT YET

HOW THE LORD ANSWERED MY PRAYER

_____
_____
_____
_____

DETAIL OF DELIVERY / LESSON LEARNED

_____
_____
_____
_____

SIGNATURE OF ACCOUNTABILITY _____

PSALM 91:8 YOU WILL ONLY OBSERVE WITH YOUR EYES
AND SEE THE PUNISHMENT OF THE WICKED.

Prayer Journal

TITLE: _____ DATE: _____ / _____ / _____

RELEVANT SCRIPTURES:

1. _____ 2. _____ 3. _____
4. _____ 5. _____ 6. _____

CONTENT OF PRAYER REQUEST

_____
_____
_____
_____

THE LORDS ANSWER WAS: DATE: _____ / _____ / _____
YES
NO
NOT YET

HOW THE LORD ANSWERED MY PRAYER

_____
_____
_____
_____

DETAIL OF DELIVERY / LESSON LEARNED

_____
_____
_____
_____

SIGNATURE OF ACCOUNTABILITY _____

Prayer Journal

TITLE: _____ DATE: _____ / _____ / _____

RELEVANT SCRIPTURES:

1. _____ 2. _____ 3. _____
4. _____ 5. _____ 6. _____

CONTENT OF PRAYER REQUEST

_____
_____
_____
_____

THE LORDS ANSWER WAS: DATE: _____ / _____ / _____
YES
NO
NOT YET

HOW THE LORD ANSWERED MY PRAYER

_____
_____
_____
_____

DETAIL OF DELIVERY / LESSON LEARNED

_____
_____
_____
_____

SIGNATURE OF ACCOUNTABILITY _____

PSALM 91:9 IF YOU SAY, "THE LORD IS MY REFUGE,"
AND YOU MAKE THE MOST HIGH YOUR DWELLING

Prayer Journal

TITLE: _____   DATE: _____ / _____ / _____

RELEVANT SCRIPTURES:

1. _____ 2. _____ 3. _____
4. _____ 5. _____ 6. _____

CONTENT OF PRAYER REQUEST

_____
_____
_____
_____

THE LORDS ANSWER WAS: DATE: _____ / _____ / _____
YES
NO
NOT YET

HOW THE LORD ANSWERED MY PRAYER

_____
_____
_____
_____

DETAIL OF DELIVERY / LESSON LEARNED

_____
_____
_____
_____

SIGNATURE OF ACCOUNTABILITY _____

Prayer Journal

TITLE: _____ DATE: _____ / _____ / _____

RELEVANT SCRIPTURES:

1. _____ 2. _____ 3. _____
4. _____ 5. _____ 6. _____

CONTENT OF PRAYER REQUEST

_____
_____
_____
_____

THE LORDS ANSWER WAS: DATE: _____ / _____ / _____
YES
NO
NOT YET

HOW THE LORD ANSWERED MY PRAYER

_____
_____
_____
_____

DETAIL OF DELIVERY / LESSON LEARNED

_____
_____
_____
_____

SIGNATURE OF ACCOUNTABILITY _____

PSALM 91:10 NO HARM WILL OVERTAKE YOU,
NO DISASTER WILL COME NEAR YOUR TENT.

Prayer Journal

TITLE: _____   DATE: _____ / _____ / _____

RELEVANT SCRIPTURES:

1. _____ 2. _____ 3. _____
4. _____ 5. _____ 6. _____

CONTENT OF PRAYER REQUEST

_____
_____
_____
_____

THE LORDS ANSWER WAS: DATE: _____ / _____ / _____
YES
NO
NOT YET

HOW THE LORD ANSWERED MY PRAYER

_____
_____
_____
_____

DETAIL OF DELIVERY / LESSON LEARNED

_____
_____
_____
_____

SIGNATURE OF ACCOUNTABILITY _____

Prayer Journal

TITLE: _____ DATE: _____ / _____ / _____

RELEVANT SCRIPTURES:

1. _____ 2. _____ 3. _____
4. _____ 5. _____ 6. _____

CONTENT OF PRAYER REQUEST

_____
_____
_____
_____

THE LORDS ANSWER WAS: DATE: _____ / _____ / _____
YES
NO
NOT YET

HOW THE LORD ANSWERED MY PRAYER

_____
_____
_____
_____

DETAIL OF DELIVERY / LESSON LEARNED

_____
_____
_____
_____

SIGNATURE OF ACCOUNTABILITY _____

PSALM 91:11 FOR HE WILL COMMAND HIS ANGELS CONCERNING YOU
TO GUARD YOU IN ALL YOUR WAYS

Prayer Journal

TITLE: _____ DATE: _____ / _____ / _____

RELEVANT SCRIPTURES:

1. _____ 2. _____ 3. _____
4. _____ 5. _____ 6. _____

CONTENT OF PRAYER REQUEST

_____
_____
_____
_____

THE LORDS ANSWER WAS: DATE: _____ / _____ / _____
YES
NO
NOT YET

HOW THE LORD ANSWERED MY PRAYER

_____
_____
_____
_____

DETAIL OF DELIVERY / LESSON LEARNED

_____
_____
_____
_____

SIGNATURE OF ACCOUNTABILITY _____

Prayer Journal

TITLE: _____ DATE: ____ / _____ / _____

RELEVANT SCRIPTURES:
1. _____ 2. _____ 3. _____
4. _____ 5. _____ 6. _____

CONTENT OF PRAYER REQUEST

_____
_____
_____
_____

THE LORDS ANSWER WAS: DATE: ____ / _____ / _____
YES
NO
NOT YET

HOW THE LORD ANSWERED MY PRAYER

_____
_____
_____
_____

DETAIL OF DELIVERY / LESSON LEARNED

_____
_____
_____
_____

SIGNATURE OF ACCOUNTABILITY _____

PSALM 91:12 THEY WILL LIFT YOU UP IN THEIR HANDS,
SO THAT YOU WILL NOT STRIKE YOUR FOOT AGAINST A STONE.

Prayer Journal

TITLE: _____ DATE: _____ / _____ / _____

RELEVANT SCRIPTURES:

1. _____ 2. _____ 3. _____
4. _____ 5. _____ 6. _____

CONTENT OF PRAYER REQUEST

_____
_____
_____
_____

THE LORDS ANSWER WAS: DATE: _____ / _____ / _____
YES
NO
NOT YET

HOW THE LORD ANSWERED MY PRAYER

_____
_____
_____
_____

DETAIL OF DELIVERY / LESSON LEARNED

_____
_____
_____
_____

SIGNATURE OF ACCOUNTABILITY _____

Prayer Journal

TITLE: _____ DATE: _____ / _____ / _____

RELEVANT SCRIPTURES:

1. _____ 2. _____ 3. _____
4. _____ 5. _____ 6. _____

CONTENT OF PRAYER REQUEST

_____
_____
_____
_____

THE LORDS ANSWER WAS: DATE: _____ / _____ / _____
YES
NO
NOT YET

HOW THE LORD ANSWERED MY PRAYER

_____
_____
_____
_____

DETAIL OF DELIVERY / LESSON LEARNED

_____
_____
_____
_____

SIGNATURE OF ACCOUNTABILITY _____

PSALM 91:13 YOU WILL TREAD ON THE LION AND THE COBRA;
YOU WILL TRAMPLE THE GREAT LION AND THE SERPENT.

Prayer Journal

TITLE: _____   DATE: _____ / _____ / _____

RELEVANT SCRIPTURES:

1. _____ 2. _____ 3. _____
4. _____ 5. _____ 6. _____

CONTENT OF PRAYER REQUEST

_____
_____
_____
_____

THE LORDS ANSWER WAS: DATE: _____ / _____ / _____
YES
NO
NOT YET

HOW THE LORD ANSWERED MY PRAYER

_____
_____
_____
_____

DETAIL OF DELIVERY / LESSON LEARNED

_____
_____
_____
_____

SIGNATURE OF ACCOUNTABILITY _____

Prayer Journal

TITLE: _____   DATE: _____ / _____ / _____

RELEVANT SCRIPTURES:

1. _____ 2. _____ 3. _____
4. _____ 5. _____ 6. _____

CONTENT OF PRAYER REQUEST

_____
_____
_____
_____

THE LORDS ANSWER WAS: DATE: _____ / _____ / _____
YES
NO
NOT YET

HOW THE LORD ANSWERED MY PRAYER

_____
_____
_____
_____

DETAIL OF DELIVERY / LESSON LEARNED

_____
_____
_____
_____

SIGNATURE OF ACCOUNTABILITY _____

PSALM 91:14 "BECAUSE HE LOVES ME," SAYS THE LORD, "I WILL RESCUE HIM;
I WILL PROTECT HIM, FOR HE ACKNOWLEDGES MY NAME.

Prayer Journal

TITLE: _____ DATE: _____ / _____ / _____

RELEVANT SCRIPTURES:

1. _____ 2. _____ 3. _____
4. _____ 5. _____ 6. _____

CONTENT OF PRAYER REQUEST

_____
_____
_____
_____

THE LORDS ANSWER WAS: DATE: _____ / _____ / _____
YES
NO
NOT YET

HOW THE LORD ANSWERED MY PRAYER

_____
_____
_____
_____

DETAIL OF DELIVERY / LESSON LEARNED

_____
_____
_____
_____

SIGNATURE OF ACCOUNTABILITY _____

Prayer Journal

TITLE: _____ DATE: _____ / _____ / _____

RELEVANT SCRIPTURES:

1. _____ 2. _____ 3. _____
4. _____ 5. _____ 6. _____

CONTENT OF PRAYER REQUEST

_____
_____
_____
_____

THE LORDS ANSWER WAS: DATE: _____ / _____ / _____
YES
NO
NOT YET

HOW THE LORD ANSWERED MY PRAYER

_____
_____
_____
_____

DETAIL OF DELIVERY / LESSON LEARNED

_____
_____
_____
_____

SIGNATURE OF ACCOUNTABILITY _____

PSALM 91:15 HE WILL CALL ON ME, AND I WILL ANSWER HIM; I WILL BE WITH HIM IN TROUBLE,
I WILL DELIVER HIM AND HONOR HIM.

Prayer Journal

TITLE: _____   DATE: _____ / _____ / _____

RELEVANT SCRIPTURES:

1. _____ 2. _____ 3. _____
4. _____ 5. _____ 6. _____

CONTENT OF PRAYER REQUEST

_____
_____
_____
_____

THE LORDS ANSWER WAS: DATE: _____ / _____ / _____
YES
NO
NOT YET

HOW THE LORD ANSWERED MY PRAYER

_____
_____
_____
_____

DETAIL OF DELIVERY / LESSON LEARNED

_____
_____
_____
_____

SIGNATURE OF ACCOUNTABILITY _____

Prayer Journal

TITLE: _____ DATE: _____ / _____ / _____

RELEVANT SCRIPTURES:

1. _____ 2. _____ 3. _____
4. _____ 5. _____ 6. _____

CONTENT OF PRAYER REQUEST

_____
_____
_____
_____

THE LORDS ANSWER WAS: DATE: _____ / _____ / _____
YES
NO
NOT YET

HOW THE LORD ANSWERED MY PRAYER

_____
_____
_____
_____

DETAIL OF DELIVERY / LESSON LEARNED

_____
_____
_____
_____

SIGNATURE OF ACCOUNTABILITY _____

PSALM 91:16 WITH LONG LIFE I WILL SATISFY HIM
AND SHOW HIM MY SALVATION."

Prayer Journal

TITLE: _____   DATE: _____ / _____ / _____

RELEVANT SCRIPTURES:

1. _____ 2. _____ 3. _____
4. _____ 5. _____ 6. _____

CONTENT OF PRAYER REQUEST

_____
_____
_____
_____

THE LORDS ANSWER WAS: DATE: _____ / _____ / _____
YES
NO
NOT YET

HOW THE LORD ANSWERED MY PRAYER

_____
_____
_____
_____

DETAIL OF DELIVERY / LESSON LEARNED

_____
_____
_____
_____

SIGNATURE OF ACCOUNTABILITY _____

Prayer Journal

TITLE: _____ DATE: _____ / _____ / _____

RELEVANT SCRIPTURES:

1. _____ 2. _____ 3. _____
4. _____ 5. _____ 6. _____

CONTENT OF PRAYER REQUEST

_____
_____
_____
_____

THE LORDS ANSWER WAS: DATE: _____ / _____ / _____
YES
NO
NOT YET

HOW THE LORD ANSWERED MY PRAYER

_____
_____
_____
_____

DETAIL OF DELIVERY / LESSON LEARNED

_____
_____
_____
_____

SIGNATURE OF ACCOUNTABILITY _____

PSALM 23:1 THE LORD IS MY SHEPHERD, I LACK NOTHING.

Prayer Journal

TITLE: _____   DATE: _____ / _____ / _____

RELEVANT SCRIPTURES:

1. _____ 2. _____ 3. _____
4. _____ 5. _____ 6. _____

CONTENT OF PRAYER REQUEST

_____
_____
_____
_____

THE LORDS ANSWER WAS: DATE: _____ / _____ / _____
YES
NO
NOT YET

HOW THE LORD ANSWERED MY PRAYER

_____
_____
_____
_____

DETAIL OF DELIVERY / LESSON LEARNED

_____
_____
_____
_____

SIGNATURE OF ACCOUNTABILITY _____

Prayer Journal

TITLE: _____ DATE: _____ / _____ / _____

RELEVANT SCRIPTURES:

1. _____ 2. _____ 3. _____
4. _____ 5. _____ 6. _____

CONTENT OF PRAYER REQUEST

_____
_____
_____
_____

THE LORDS ANSWER WAS: DATE: _____ / _____ / _____
YES
NO
NOT YET

HOW THE LORD ANSWERED MY PRAYER

_____
_____
_____
_____

DETAIL OF DELIVERY / LESSON LEARNED

_____
_____
_____
_____

SIGNATURE OF ACCOUNTABILITY _____

PSALM 23:2 HE MAKES ME LIE DOWN IN GREEN PASTURES,
HE LEADS ME BESIDE QUIET WATERS

Prayer Journal

TITLE: _____ DATE: _____ / _____ / _____

RELEVANT SCRIPTURES:

1. _____ 2. _____ 3. _____
4. _____ 5. _____ 6. _____

CONTENT OF PRAYER REQUEST

_____
_____
_____
_____

THE LORDS ANSWER WAS: DATE: _____ / _____ / _____
YES
NO
NOT YET

HOW THE LORD ANSWERED MY PRAYER

_____
_____
_____
_____

DETAIL OF DELIVERY / LESSON LEARNED

_____
_____
_____
_____

SIGNATURE OF ACCOUNTABILITY _____

Prayer Journal

TITLE: _____ DATE: _____ / _____ / _____

RELEVANT SCRIPTURES:

1. _____ 2. _____ 3. _____
4. _____ 5. _____ 6. _____

CONTENT OF PRAYER REQUEST

_____
_____
_____
_____

THE LORDS ANSWER WAS: DATE: _____ / _____ / _____
YES
NO
NOT YET

HOW THE LORD ANSWERED MY PRAYER

_____
_____
_____
_____

DETAIL OF DELIVERY / LESSON LEARNED

_____
_____
_____
_____

SIGNATURE OF ACCOUNTABILITY _____

PSALM 23:3 HE REFRESHES MY SOUL. HE GUIDES ME ALONG THE RIGHT PATHS FOR HIS NAME'S SAKE.

Prayer Journal

TITLE: _____   DATE: _____ / _____ / _____

RELEVANT SCRIPTURES:

1. _____ 2. _____ 3. _____
4. _____ 5. _____ 6. _____

CONTENT OF PRAYER REQUEST

_____
_____
_____
_____

THE LORDS ANSWER WAS: DATE: _____ / _____ / _____
YES
NO
NOT YET

HOW THE LORD ANSWERED MY PRAYER

_____
_____
_____
_____

DETAIL OF DELIVERY / LESSON LEARNED

_____
_____
_____
_____

SIGNATURE OF ACCOUNTABILITY _____

Prayer Journal

TITLE: _____ DATE: _____ / _____ / _____

RELEVANT SCRIPTURES:

1. _____ 2. _____ 3. _____
4. _____ 5. _____ 6. _____

CONTENT OF PRAYER REQUEST

_____
_____
_____
_____

THE LORDS ANSWER WAS: DATE: _____ / _____ / _____
YES
NO
NOT YET

HOW THE LORD ANSWERED MY PRAYER

_____
_____
_____
_____

DETAIL OF DELIVERY / LESSON LEARNED

_____
_____
_____
_____

SIGNATURE OF ACCOUNTABILITY _____

PSALM 23:4 EVEN THOUGH I WALK THROUGH THE DARKEST VALLEY, I WILL FEAR NO EVIL, FOR YOU ARE WITH ME; YOUR ROD AND YOUR STAFF, THEY COMFORT ME.

Prayer Journal

TITLE: _____ DATE: _____ / _____ / _____

RELEVANT SCRIPTURES:

1. _____ 2. _____ 3. _____
4. _____ 5. _____ 6. _____

CONTENT OF PRAYER REQUEST

_____
_____
_____
_____

THE LORDS ANSWER WAS:　　　　　DATE: _____ / _____ / _____
YES
NO
NOT YET

HOW THE LORD ANSWERED MY PRAYER

_____
_____
_____
_____

DETAIL OF DELIVERY / LESSON LEARNED

_____
_____
_____
_____

SIGNATURE OF ACCOUNTABILITY _____

Prayer Journal

TITLE: _____   DATE: _____ / _____ / _____

RELEVANT SCRIPTURES:

1. _____ 2. _____ 3. _____
4. _____ 5. _____ 6. _____

CONTENT OF PRAYER REQUEST

_____
_____
_____
_____

THE LORDS ANSWER WAS: DATE: _____ / _____ / _____
YES
NO
NOT YET

HOW THE LORD ANSWERED MY PRAYER

_____
_____
_____
_____

DETAIL OF DELIVERY / LESSON LEARNED

_____
_____
_____
_____

SIGNATURE OF ACCOUNTABILITY _____

PSALM 23:5 YOU PREPARE A TABLE BEFORE ME IN THE PRESENCE OF MY ENEMIES.
YOU ANOINT MY HEAD WITH OIL; MY CUP OVERFLOWS.

Prayer Journal

TITLE: _____   DATE: _____ / _____ / _____

RELEVANT SCRIPTURES:

1. _____ 2. _____ 3. _____
4. _____ 5. _____ 6. _____

CONTENT OF PRAYER REQUEST

_____
_____
_____
_____

THE LORDS ANSWER WAS: DATE: _____ / _____ / _____
YES
NO
NOT YET

HOW THE LORD ANSWERED MY PRAYER

_____
_____
_____
_____

DETAIL OF DELIVERY / LESSON LEARNED

_____
_____
_____
_____

SIGNATURE OF ACCOUNTABILITY _____

Prayer Journal

TITLE: _____   DATE: _____ / _____ / _____

RELEVANT SCRIPTURES:

1. _____ 2. _____ 3. _____
4. _____ 5. _____ 6. _____

CONTENT OF PRAYER REQUEST

_____
_____
_____
_____

THE LORDS ANSWER WAS: DATE: _____ / _____ / _____
YES
NO
NOT YET

HOW THE LORD ANSWERED MY PRAYER

_____
_____
_____
_____

DETAIL OF DELIVERY / LESSON LEARNED

_____
_____
_____
_____

SIGNATURE OF ACCOUNTABILITY _____

PSALM 23:6 SURELY YOUR GOODNESS AND LOVE WILL FOLLOW ME ALL THE DAYS OF MY LIFE, AND I WILL DWELL IN THE HOUSE OF THE LORD FOREVER.

Prayer Journal

TITLE: _____ DATE: _____ / _____ / _____

RELEVANT SCRIPTURES:

1. _____ 2. _____ 3. _____
4. _____ 5. _____ 6. _____

CONTENT OF PRAYER REQUEST

_____
_____
_____
_____

THE LORDS ANSWER WAS: DATE: _____ / _____ / _____
YES
NO
NOT YET

HOW THE LORD ANSWERED MY PRAYER

_____
_____
_____
_____

DETAIL OF DELIVERY / LESSON LEARNED

_____
_____
_____
_____

SIGNATURE OF ACCOUNTABILITY _____

Prayer Journal

TITLE: _____ DATE: _____ / _____ / _____

RELEVANT SCRIPTURES:

1. _____ 2. _____ 3. _____
4. _____ 5. _____ 6. _____

CONTENT OF PRAYER REQUEST

_____
_____
_____
_____

THE LORDS ANSWER WAS: DATE: _____ / _____ / _____
YES
NO
NOT YET

HOW THE LORD ANSWERED MY PRAYER

_____
_____
_____
_____

DETAIL OF DELIVERY / LESSON LEARNED

_____
_____
_____
_____

SIGNATURE OF ACCOUNTABILITY _____

Prayer Journal

TITLE: _____ DATE: _____ / _____ / _____

RELEVANT SCRIPTURES:

1. _____ 2. _____ 3. _____
4. _____ 5. _____ 6. _____

CONTENT OF PRAYER REQUEST

_____
_____
_____
_____

THE LORDS ANSWER WAS: DATE: _____ / _____ / _____
YES
NO
NOT YET

HOW THE LORD ANSWERED MY PRAYER

_____
_____
_____
_____

DETAIL OF DELIVERY / LESSON LEARNED

_____
_____
_____
_____

SIGNATURE OF ACCOUNTABILITY _____

Prayer Journal

TITLE: _____ DATE: _____ / _____ / _____

RELEVANT SCRIPTURES:

1. _____ 2. _____ 3. _____
4. _____ 5. _____ 6. _____

CONTENT OF PRAYER REQUEST

_____
_____
_____
_____

THE LORDS ANSWER WAS: DATE: _____ / _____ / _____
YES
NO
NOT YET

HOW THE LORD ANSWERED MY PRAYER

_____
_____
_____
_____

DETAIL OF DELIVERY / LESSON LEARNED

_____
_____
_____
_____

SIGNATURE OF ACCOUNTABILITY _____

Prayer Journal

TITLE: _____ DATE: _____ / _____ / _____

RELEVANT SCRIPTURES:

1. _____ 2. _____ 3. _____
4. _____ 5. _____ 6. _____

CONTENT OF PRAYER REQUEST

_____
_____
_____
_____

THE LORDS ANSWER WAS: DATE: _____ / _____ / _____
YES
NO
NOT YET

HOW THE LORD ANSWERED MY PRAYER

_____
_____
_____
_____

DETAIL OF DELIVERY / LESSON LEARNED

_____
_____
_____
_____

SIGNATURE OF ACCOUNTABILITY _____

Prayer Journal

TITLE: _____ DATE: _____ / _____ / _____

RELEVANT SCRIPTURES:

1. _____ 2. _____ 3. _____
4. _____ 5. _____ 6. _____

CONTENT OF PRAYER REQUEST

_____
_____
_____
_____

THE LORDS ANSWER WAS: DATE: _____ / _____ / _____
YES
NO
NOT YET

HOW THE LORD ANSWERED MY PRAYER

_____
_____
_____
_____

DETAIL OF DELIVERY / LESSON LEARNED

_____
_____
_____
_____

SIGNATURE OF ACCOUNTABILITY _____

Prayer Journal

TITLE: _____ DATE: _____ / _____ / _____

RELEVANT SCRIPTURES:

1. _____ 2. _____ 3. _____
4. _____ 5. _____ 6. _____

CONTENT OF PRAYER REQUEST

_____
_____
_____
_____

THE LORDS ANSWER WAS: DATE: _____ / _____ / _____
YES
NO
NOT YET

HOW THE LORD ANSWERED MY PRAYER

_____
_____
_____
_____

DETAIL OF DELIVERY / LESSON LEARNED

_____
_____
_____
_____

SIGNATURE OF ACCOUNTABILITY _____

Prayer Journal

TITLE: _____ DATE: _____ / _____ / _____

RELEVANT SCRIPTURES:

1. _____ 2. _____ 3. _____
4. _____ 5. _____ 6. _____

CONTENT OF PRAYER REQUEST

_____
_____
_____
_____

THE LORDS ANSWER WAS: DATE: _____ / _____ / _____
YES
NO
NOT YET

HOW THE LORD ANSWERED MY PRAYER

_____
_____
_____
_____

DETAIL OF DELIVERY / LESSON LEARNED

_____
_____
_____
_____

SIGNATURE OF ACCOUNTABILITY _____

Prayer Journal

TITLE: _____   DATE: _____ / _____ / _____

RELEVANT SCRIPTURES:

1. _____ 2. _____ 3. _____
4. _____ 5. _____ 6. _____

CONTENT OF PRAYER REQUEST

_____
_____
_____
_____

THE LORDS ANSWER WAS: DATE: _____ / _____ / _____
YES
NO
NOT YET

HOW THE LORD ANSWERED MY PRAYER

_____
_____
_____
_____

DETAIL OF DELIVERY / LESSON LEARNED

_____
_____
_____
_____

SIGNATURE OF ACCOUNTABILITY _____

Prayer Journal

TITLE: _____   DATE: _____ / _____ / _____

RELEVANT SCRIPTURES:

1. _____ 2. _____ 3. _____
4. _____ 5. _____ 6. _____

CONTENT OF PRAYER REQUEST

_____
_____
_____
_____

THE LORDS ANSWER WAS: DATE: _____ / _____ / _____
YES
NO
NOT YET

HOW THE LORD ANSWERED MY PRAYER

_____
_____
_____
_____

DETAIL OF DELIVERY / LESSON LEARNED

_____
_____
_____
_____

SIGNATURE OF ACCOUNTABILITY _____

Prayer Journal

TITLE: _____ DATE: _____ / _____ / _____

RELEVANT SCRIPTURES:

1. _____ 2. _____ 3. _____
4. _____ 5. _____ 6. _____

CONTENT OF PRAYER REQUEST

_____
_____
_____
_____

THE LORDS ANSWER WAS: DATE: _____ / _____ / _____
YES
NO
NOT YET

HOW THE LORD ANSWERED MY PRAYER

_____
_____
_____
_____

DETAIL OF DELIVERY / LESSON LEARNED

_____
_____
_____
_____

SIGNATURE OF ACCOUNTABILITY _____

Prayer Journal

TITLE: _____   DATE: _____ / _____ / _____

RELEVANT SCRIPTURES:
1. _____ 2. _____ 3. _____
4. _____ 5. _____ 6. _____

CONTENT OF PRAYER REQUEST

_____
_____
_____
_____

THE LORDS ANSWER WAS: DATE: _____ / _____ / _____
YES
NO
NOT YET

HOW THE LORD ANSWERED MY PRAYER

_____
_____
_____
_____

DETAIL OF DELIVERY / LESSON LEARNED

_____
_____
_____
_____

SIGNATURE OF ACCOUNTABILITY _____

Prayer Journal

TITLE: _____ DATE: _____ / _____ / _____

RELEVANT SCRIPTURES:

1. _____ 2. _____ 3. _____
4. _____ 5. _____ 6. _____

CONTENT OF PRAYER REQUEST

_____
_____
_____
_____

THE LORDS ANSWER WAS: DATE: _____ / _____ / _____
YES
NO
NOT YET

HOW THE LORD ANSWERED MY PRAYER

_____
_____
_____
_____

DETAIL OF DELIVERY / LESSON LEARNED

_____
_____
_____
_____

SIGNATURE OF ACCOUNTABILITY _____

Prayer Journal

TITLE: _____ DATE: _____ / _____ / _____

RELEVANT SCRIPTURES:

1. _____ 2. _____ 3. _____
4. _____ 5. _____ 6. _____

CONTENT OF PRAYER REQUEST

_____
_____
_____
_____

THE LORDS ANSWER WAS: DATE: _____ / _____ / _____
YES
NO
NOT YET

HOW THE LORD ANSWERED MY PRAYER

_____
_____
_____
_____

DETAIL OF DELIVERY / LESSON LEARNED

_____
_____
_____
_____

SIGNATURE OF ACCOUNTABILITY _____

Prayer Journal

TITLE: _____   DATE: _____ / _____ / _____

RELEVANT SCRIPTURES:
1. _____ 2. _____ 3. _____
4. _____ 5. _____ 6. _____

CONTENT OF PRAYER REQUEST
_____
_____
_____
_____

THE LORDS ANSWER WAS: DATE: _____ / _____ / _____
YES
NO
NOT YET

HOW THE LORD ANSWERED MY PRAYER
_____
_____
_____
_____

DETAIL OF DELIVERY / LESSON LEARNED
_____
_____
_____
_____

SIGNATURE OF ACCOUNTABILITY _____

Prayer Journal

TITLE: _____   DATE: _____ / _____ / _____

RELEVANT SCRIPTURES:

1. _____ 2. _____ 3. _____
4. _____ 5. _____ 6. _____

CONTENT OF PRAYER REQUEST

_____
_____
_____
_____

THE LORDS ANSWER WAS: DATE: _____ / _____ / _____
YES
NO
NOT YET

HOW THE LORD ANSWERED MY PRAYER

_____
_____
_____
_____

DETAIL OF DELIVERY / LESSON LEARNED

_____
_____
_____
_____

SIGNATURE OF ACCOUNTABILITY _____

Prayer Journal

TITLE: _____   DATE: _____ / _____ / _____

RELEVANT SCRIPTURES:

1. _____ 2. _____ 3. _____
4. _____ 5. _____ 6. _____

CONTENT OF PRAYER REQUEST

_____
_____
_____
_____

THE LORDS ANSWER WAS: DATE: _____ / _____ / _____
YES
NO
NOT YET

HOW THE LORD ANSWERED MY PRAYER

_____
_____
_____
_____

DETAIL OF DELIVERY / LESSON LEARNED

_____
_____
_____
_____

SIGNATURE OF ACCOUNTABILITY _____

Prayer Journal

TITLE: _____ DATE: _____ / _____ / _____

RELEVANT SCRIPTURES:

1. _____ 2. _____ 3. _____
4. _____ 5. _____ 6. _____

CONTENT OF PRAYER REQUEST

_____
_____
_____
_____

THE LORDS ANSWER WAS: DATE: _____ / _____ / _____
YES
NO
NOT YET

HOW THE LORD ANSWERED MY PRAYER

_____
_____
_____
_____

DETAIL OF DELIVERY / LESSON LEARNED

_____
_____
_____
_____

SIGNATURE OF ACCOUNTABILITY _____

Prayer Journal

TITLE: _____   DATE: _____ / _____ / _____

RELEVANT SCRIPTURES:

1. _____ 2. _____ 3. _____
4. _____ 5. _____ 6. _____

CONTENT OF PRAYER REQUEST

_____
_____
_____
_____

THE LORDS ANSWER WAS: DATE: _____ / _____ / _____
YES
NO
NOT YET

HOW THE LORD ANSWERED MY PRAYER

_____
_____
_____
_____

DETAIL OF DELIVERY / LESSON LEARNED

_____
_____
_____
_____

SIGNATURE OF ACCOUNTABILITY _____

Prayer Journal

TITLE: _____ DATE: _____ / _____ / _____

RELEVANT SCRIPTURES:

1. _____ 2. _____ 3. _____
4. _____ 5. _____ 6. _____

CONTENT OF PRAYER REQUEST

_____
_____
_____
_____

THE LORDS ANSWER WAS: DATE: _____ / _____ / _____
YES
NO
NOT YET

HOW THE LORD ANSWERED MY PRAYER

_____
_____
_____
_____

DETAIL OF DELIVERY / LESSON LEARNED

_____
_____
_____
_____

SIGNATURE OF ACCOUNTABILITY _____

Prayer Journal

TITLE: _____ DATE: _____ / _____ / _____

RELEVANT SCRIPTURES:

1. _____ 2. _____ 3. _____
4. _____ 5. _____ 6. _____

CONTENT OF PRAYER REQUEST

_____
_____
_____
_____

THE LORDS ANSWER WAS: DATE: _____ / _____ / _____
YES
NO
NOT YET

HOW THE LORD ANSWERED MY PRAYER

_____
_____
_____
_____

DETAIL OF DELIVERY / LESSON LEARNED

_____
_____
_____
_____

SIGNATURE OF ACCOUNTABILITY _____

Prayer Journal

TITLE: _____   DATE: _____ / _____ / _____

RELEVANT SCRIPTURES:

1. _____ 2. _____ 3. _____
4. _____ 5. _____ 6. _____

CONTENT OF PRAYER REQUEST

_____
_____
_____
_____

THE LORDS ANSWER WAS: DATE: _____ / _____ / _____
YES
NO
NOT YET

HOW THE LORD ANSWERED MY PRAYER

_____
_____
_____
_____

DETAIL OF DELIVERY / LESSON LEARNED

_____
_____
_____
_____

SIGNATURE OF ACCOUNTABILITY _____

Prayer Journal

TITLE: _____ DATE: _____ / _____ / _____

RELEVANT SCRIPTURES:

1. _____ 2. _____ 3. _____
4. _____ 5. _____ 6. _____

CONTENT OF PRAYER REQUEST

_____
_____
_____
_____

THE LORDS ANSWER WAS: DATE: _____ / _____ / _____
YES
NO
NOT YET

HOW THE LORD ANSWERED MY PRAYER

_____
_____
_____
_____

DETAIL OF DELIVERY / LESSON LEARNED

_____
_____
_____
_____

SIGNATURE OF ACCOUNTABILITY _____

Prayer Journal

TITLE: _____ DATE: _____ / _____ / _____

RELEVANT SCRIPTURES:

1. _____ 2. _____ 3. _____
4. _____ 5. _____ 6. _____

CONTENT OF PRAYER REQUEST

_____
_____
_____
_____

THE LORDS ANSWER WAS: DATE: _____ / _____ / _____
YES
NO
NOT YET

HOW THE LORD ANSWERED MY PRAYER

_____
_____
_____
_____

DETAIL OF DELIVERY / LESSON LEARNED

_____
_____
_____
_____

SIGNATURE OF ACCOUNTABILITY _____

Prayer Journal

TITLE: _____ DATE: _____ / _____ / _____

RELEVANT SCRIPTURES:

1. _____ 2. _____ 3. _____
4. _____ 5. _____ 6. _____

CONTENT OF PRAYER REQUEST

_____
_____
_____
_____

THE LORDS ANSWER WAS: DATE: _____ / _____ / _____
YES
NO
NOT YET

HOW THE LORD ANSWERED MY PRAYER

_____
_____
_____
_____

DETAIL OF DELIVERY / LESSON LEARNED

_____
_____
_____
_____

SIGNATURE OF ACCOUNTABILITY _____

Prayer Journal

TITLE: _____ DATE: _____ / _____ / _____

RELEVANT SCRIPTURES:

1. _____ 2. _____ 3. _____
4. _____ 5. _____ 6. _____

CONTENT OF PRAYER REQUEST

_____
_____
_____
_____

THE LORDS ANSWER WAS: DATE: _____ / _____ / _____
YES
NO
NOT YET

HOW THE LORD ANSWERED MY PRAYER

_____
_____
_____
_____

DETAIL OF DELIVERY / LESSON LEARNED

_____
_____
_____
_____

SIGNATURE OF ACCOUNTABILITY _____

Prayer Journal

TITLE: _____ DATE: _____ / _____ / _____

RELEVANT SCRIPTURES:

1. _____ 2. _____ 3. _____
4. _____ 5. _____ 6. _____

CONTENT OF PRAYER REQUEST

_____
_____
_____
_____

THE LORDS ANSWER WAS: DATE: _____ / _____ / _____
YES
NO
NOT YET

HOW THE LORD ANSWERED MY PRAYER

_____
_____
_____
_____

DETAIL OF DELIVERY / LESSON LEARNED

_____
_____
_____
_____

SIGNATURE OF ACCOUNTABILITY _____

Prayer Journal

TITLE: _____ DATE: _____ / _____ / _____

RELEVANT SCRIPTURES:

1. _____ 2. _____ 3. _____
4. _____ 5. _____ 6. _____

CONTENT OF PRAYER REQUEST

_____
_____
_____
_____

THE LORDS ANSWER WAS: DATE: _____ / _____ / _____
YES
NO
NOT YET

HOW THE LORD ANSWERED MY PRAYER

_____
_____
_____
_____

DETAIL OF DELIVERY / LESSON LEARNED

_____
_____
_____
_____

SIGNATURE OF ACCOUNTABILITY _____

Prayer Journal

TITLE: _____ DATE: _____ / _____ / _____

RELEVANT SCRIPTURES:

1. _____ 2. _____ 3. _____
4. _____ 5. _____ 6. _____

CONTENT OF PRAYER REQUEST

_____
_____
_____
_____

THE LORDS ANSWER WAS: DATE: _____ / _____ / _____
YES
NO
NOT YET

HOW THE LORD ANSWERED MY PRAYER

_____
_____
_____
_____

DETAIL OF DELIVERY / LESSON LEARNED

_____
_____
_____
_____

SIGNATURE OF ACCOUNTABILITY _____

Prayer Journal

TITLE: _____ DATE: _____ / _____ / _____

RELEVANT SCRIPTURES:

1. _____ 2. _____ 3. _____
4. _____ 5. _____ 6. _____

CONTENT OF PRAYER REQUEST

_____
_____
_____
_____

THE LORDS ANSWER WAS:　　　　　DATE: _____ / _____ / _____
YES
NO
NOT YET

HOW THE LORD ANSWERED MY PRAYER

_____
_____
_____
_____

DETAIL OF DELIVERY / LESSON LEARNED

_____
_____
_____
_____

SIGNATURE OF ACCOUNTABILITY _____

Take Us To Church

Prayer Journal

TITLE: _____ DATE: ___/___/____

SPEAKER: _____

SERMON: _____ BOOK OF: _____

SERMON NOTES:

_____
_____
_____
_____
_____
_____
_____
_____

PERSONAL REFLECTIONS:

_____
_____
_____
_____
_____
_____
_____
_____
_____
_____
_____

Prayer Journal

TITLE: _____ DATE: ___/___/___

SPEAKER: _____

SERMON: _____ BOOK OF: _____

SERMON NOTES:
_____
_____
_____
_____
_____
_____
_____
_____

PERSONAL REFLECTIONS:
_____
_____
_____
_____
_____
_____
_____
_____
_____
_____

Prayer Journal

TITLE: _____ DATE: ___/___/____

SPEAKER: _____

SERMON: _____ BOOK OF: _____

SERMON NOTES:
_____
_____
_____
_____
_____
_____
_____
_____

PERSONAL REFLECTIONS:
_____
_____
_____
_____
_____
_____
_____
_____
_____
_____

Prayer Journal

TITLE: _____ DATE: ___/___/___

SPEAKER: _____

SERMON: _____ BOOK OF: _____

SERMON NOTES:
_____
_____
_____
_____
_____
_____
_____
_____

PERSONAL REFLECTIONS:
_____
_____
_____
_____
_____
_____
_____
_____
_____
_____

Prayer Journal

TITLE: _____ DATE: ___/___/___

SPEAKER: _____

SERMON: _____ BOOK OF: _____

SERMON NOTES:
_____
_____
_____
_____
_____
_____
_____
_____

PERSONAL REFLECTIONS:
_____
_____
_____
_____
_____
_____
_____
_____
_____

Prayer Journal

TITLE: _____ DATE: ___/___/____

SPEAKER: _____

SERMON: _____ BOOK OF: _____

SERMON NOTES:
_____
_____
_____
_____
_____
_____
_____
_____

PERSONAL REFLECTIONS:
_____
_____
_____
_____
_____
_____
_____
_____
_____
_____
_____

Prayer Journal

TITLE: _____ DATE: ___/___/____

SPEAKER: _____

SERMON: _____ BOOK OF: _____

SERMON NOTES:
_____
_____
_____
_____
_____
_____
_____
_____

PERSONAL REFLECTIONS:
_____
_____
_____
_____
_____
_____
_____
_____
_____
_____

Prayer Journal

TITLE: _____ DATE: ___/___/___

SPEAKER: _____

SERMON: _____ BOOK OF: _____

SERMON NOTES:
_____
_____
_____
_____
_____
_____
_____

PERSONAL REFLECTIONS:
_____
_____
_____
_____
_____
_____
_____
_____
_____
_____

Prayer Journal

TITLE: _____ DATE: ___/___/____

SPEAKER: _____

SERMON: _____ BOOK OF: _____

SERMON NOTES:

_____
_____
_____
_____
_____
_____
_____

PERSONAL REFLECTIONS:

_____
_____
_____
_____
_____
_____
_____
_____
_____
_____

Prayer Journal

TITLE: _____ DATE: ___/___/___

SPEAKER: _____

SERMON: _____ BOOK OF: _____

SERMON NOTES:
_____
_____
_____
_____
_____
_____
_____
_____

PERSONAL REFLECTIONS:
_____
_____
_____
_____
_____
_____
_____
_____
_____
_____

Prayer Journal

TITLE: _____ **DATE:** ___/___/___

SPEAKER: _____

SERMON: _____ **BOOK OF:** _____

SERMON NOTES:
_____
_____
_____
_____
_____
_____
_____
_____

PERSONAL REFLECTIONS:
_____
_____
_____
_____
_____
_____
_____
_____
_____
_____
_____

Prayer Journal

TITLE: _____ DATE: ___/___/____

SPEAKER: _____

SERMON: _____ BOOK OF: _____

SERMON NOTES:
_____
_____
_____
_____
_____
_____
_____
_____

PERSONAL REFLECTIONS:
_____
_____
_____
_____
_____
_____
_____
_____
_____
_____
_____

Prayer Journal

TITLE: _____ **DATE:** ___/___/___

SPEAKER: _____

SERMON: _____ **BOOK OF:** _____

SERMON NOTES:
_____
_____
_____
_____
_____
_____
_____
_____

PERSONAL REFLECTIONS:
_____
_____
_____
_____
_____
_____
_____
_____
_____
_____

Prayer Journal

TITLE: _____ DATE: ___/___/___

SPEAKER: _____

SERMON: _____ BOOK OF: _____

SERMON NOTES:
_____
_____
_____
_____
_____
_____
_____
_____

PERSONAL REFLECTIONS:
_____
_____
_____
_____
_____
_____
_____
_____
_____

Prayer Journal

TITLE: _____ DATE: ___/___/____

SPEAKER: _____

SERMON: _____ BOOK OF: _____

SERMON NOTES:

_____
_____
_____
_____
_____
_____
_____

PERSONAL REFLECTIONS:

_____
_____
_____
_____
_____
_____
_____
_____
_____

Prayer Journal

TITLE: _____ DATE: ___/___/____

SPEAKER: _____

SERMON: _____ BOOK OF: _____

SERMON NOTES:
_____
_____
_____
_____
_____
_____
_____

PERSONAL REFLECTIONS:
_____
_____
_____
_____
_____
_____
_____
_____
_____
_____

Prayer Journal

TITLE: _____ DATE: ___/___/___

SPEAKER: _____

SERMON: _____ BOOK OF: _____

SERMON NOTES:
_____
_____
_____
_____
_____
_____
_____
_____

PERSONAL REFLECTIONS:
_____
_____
_____
_____
_____
_____
_____
_____
_____
_____

Prayer Journal

TITLE: _____ DATE: ___/___/____

SPEAKER: _____

SERMON: _____ BOOK OF: _____

SERMON NOTES:
_____
_____
_____
_____
_____
_____
_____
_____

PERSONAL REFLECTIONS:
_____
_____
_____
_____
_____
_____
_____
_____
_____
_____

Prayer Journal

TITLE: _____ DATE: ___/___/___

SPEAKER: _____

SERMON: _____ BOOK OF: _____

SERMON NOTES:

_____
_____
_____
_____
_____
_____
_____
_____
_____

PERSONAL REFLECTIONS:

_____
_____
_____
_____
_____
_____
_____
_____
_____
_____

Prayer Journal

TITLE: _____ DATE: ___/___/___

SPEAKER: _____

SERMON: _____ BOOK OF: _____

SERMON NOTES:
_____
_____
_____
_____
_____
_____
_____
_____

PERSONAL REFLECTIONS:
_____
_____
_____
_____
_____
_____
_____
_____
_____
_____
_____
_____

Prayer Journal

TITLE: _____ DATE: ___/___/____

SPEAKER: _____

SERMON: _____ BOOK OF: _____

SERMON NOTES:

_____
_____
_____
_____
_____
_____
_____
_____

PERSONAL REFLECTIONS:

_____
_____
_____
_____
_____
_____
_____
_____
_____
_____

Prayer Journal

TITLE: _____ DATE: ___/___/____

SPEAKER: _____

SERMON: _____ BOOK OF: _____

SERMON NOTES:
_____
_____
_____
_____
_____
_____
_____
_____

PERSONAL REFLECTIONS:
_____
_____
_____
_____
_____
_____
_____
_____
_____
_____

Prayer Journal

TITLE: _____ DATE: ___/___/___

SPEAKER: _____

SERMON: _____ BOOK OF: _____

SERMON NOTES:
_____
_____
_____
_____
_____
_____
_____
_____

PERSONAL REFLECTIONS:
_____
_____
_____
_____
_____
_____
_____
_____
_____
_____

Prayer Journal

TITLE: _____ DATE: ___/___/___

SPEAKER: _____

SERMON: _____ BOOK OF: _____

SERMON NOTES:
_____
_____
_____
_____
_____
_____
_____
_____

PERSONAL REFLECTIONS:
_____
_____
_____
_____
_____
_____
_____
_____
_____
_____
_____

Prayer Journal

TITLE: _____ DATE: ___/___/___

SPEAKER: _____

SERMON: _____ BOOK OF: _____

SERMON NOTES:
_____
_____
_____
_____
_____
_____
_____
_____

PERSONAL REFLECTIONS:
_____
_____
_____
_____
_____
_____
_____
_____
_____
_____

Prayer Journal

TITLE: _____ DATE: ___/___/____

SPEAKER: _____

SERMON: _____ BOOK OF: _____

SERMON NOTES:
_____
_____
_____
_____
_____
_____
_____

PERSONAL REFLECTIONS:
_____
_____
_____
_____
_____
_____
_____
_____
_____

Prayer Journal

TITLE: _____ DATE: ___/___/____

SPEAKER: _____

SERMON: _____ BOOK OF: _____

SERMON NOTES:

_____
_____
_____
_____
_____
_____
_____

PERSONAL REFLECTIONS:

_____
_____
_____
_____
_____
_____
_____
_____
_____

Prayer Journal

TITLE: _____ DATE: ___/___/____

SPEAKER: _____

SERMON: _____ BOOK OF: _____

SERMON NOTES:

_____
_____
_____
_____
_____
_____
_____
_____

PERSONAL REFLECTIONS:

_____
_____
_____
_____
_____
_____
_____
_____
_____
_____

Prayer Journal

TITLE: _____ DATE: ___/___/____

SPEAKER: _____

SERMON: _____ BOOK OF: _____

SERMON NOTES:
_____
_____
_____
_____
_____
_____
_____

PERSONAL REFLECTIONS:
_____
_____
_____
_____
_____
_____
_____
_____
_____
_____

Prayer Journal

TITLE: _____ DATE: ___/___/___

SPEAKER: _____

SERMON: _____ BOOK OF: _____

SERMON NOTES:
_____
_____
_____
_____
_____
_____
_____
_____

PERSONAL REFLECTIONS:
_____
_____
_____
_____
_____
_____
_____
_____
_____
_____

Prayer Journal

TITLE: _____ DATE: ___/___/____

SPEAKER: _____

SERMON: _____ BOOK OF: _____

SERMON NOTES:

_____
_____
_____
_____
_____
_____
_____

PERSONAL REFLECTIONS:

_____
_____
_____
_____
_____
_____
_____
_____

Prayer Journal

TITLE: _____ DATE: ___/___/____

SPEAKER: _____

SERMON: _____ BOOK OF: _____

SERMON NOTES:
_____
_____
_____
_____
_____
_____
_____
_____

PERSONAL REFLECTIONS:
_____
_____
_____
_____
_____
_____
_____
_____
_____
_____

Prayer Journal

TITLE: _____ DATE: ___/___/____

SPEAKER: _____

SERMON: _____ BOOK OF: _____

SERMON NOTES:

_____
_____
_____
_____
_____
_____
_____

PERSONAL REFLECTIONS:

_____
_____
_____
_____
_____
_____
_____
_____
_____
_____

Prayer Journal

TITLE: _____ DATE: ___/___/____

SPEAKER: _____

SERMON: _____ BOOK OF: _____

SERMON NOTES:
_____
_____
_____
_____
_____
_____
_____
_____

PERSONAL REFLECTIONS:
_____
_____
_____
_____
_____
_____
_____
_____
_____
_____

Prayer Journal

TITLE: _____ DATE: ___/___/___

SPEAKER: _____

SERMON: _____ BOOK OF: _____

SERMON NOTES:
_____
_____
_____
_____
_____
_____
_____
_____

PERSONAL REFLECTIONS:
_____
_____
_____
_____
_____
_____
_____
_____
_____
_____

Prayer Journal

TITLE: _____ DATE: ___/___/___

SPEAKER: _____

SERMON: _____ BOOK OF: _____

SERMON NOTES:
_____
_____
_____
_____
_____
_____
_____
_____

PERSONAL REFLECTIONS:
_____
_____
_____
_____
_____
_____
_____
_____
_____
_____

Prayer Journal

TITLE: _____ DATE: ___/___/___

SPEAKER: _____

SERMON: _____ BOOK OF: _____

SERMON NOTES:

_____
_____
_____
_____
_____
_____
_____
_____

PERSONAL REFLECTIONS:

_____
_____
_____
_____
_____
_____
_____
_____
_____
_____

Prayer Journal

TITLE: _____ DATE: ___/___/___

SPEAKER: _____

SERMON: _____ BOOK OF: _____

SERMON NOTES:
_____
_____
_____
_____
_____
_____
_____
_____

PERSONAL REFLECTIONS:
_____
_____
_____
_____
_____
_____
_____
_____
_____
_____
_____
_____

Prayer Journal

TITLE: _____ DATE: ___/___/___

SPEAKER: _____

SERMON: _____ BOOK OF: _____

SERMON NOTES:

_____
_____
_____
_____
_____
_____
_____

PERSONAL REFLECTIONS:

_____
_____
_____
_____
_____
_____
_____
_____
_____

Prayer Journal

TITLE: _____ DATE: ___/___/____

SPEAKER: _____

SERMON: _____ BOOK OF: _____

SERMON NOTES:
_____
_____
_____
_____
_____
_____
_____
_____

PERSONAL REFLECTIONS:
_____
_____
_____
_____
_____
_____
_____
_____
_____

Prayer Journal

TITLE: _____ DATE: ___/___/___

SPEAKER: _____

SERMON: _____ BOOK OF: _____

SERMON NOTES:

_____
_____
_____
_____
_____
_____
_____

PERSONAL REFLECTIONS:

_____
_____
_____
_____
_____
_____
_____
_____
_____
_____

Prayer Journal

TITLE: _____ DATE: ___/___/___

SPEAKER: _____

SERMON: _____ BOOK OF: _____

SERMON NOTES:
_____
_____
_____
_____
_____
_____
_____

PERSONAL REFLECTIONS:
_____
_____
_____
_____
_____
_____
_____
_____
_____
_____

Prayer Journal

TITLE: _____ DATE: ___/___/___

SPEAKER: _____

SERMON:_____ BOOK OF:_____

SERMON NOTES:

_____
_____
_____
_____
_____
_____
_____
_____

PERSONAL REFLECTIONS:

_____
_____
_____
_____
_____
_____
_____
_____
_____
_____

Prayer Journal

TITLE: _____ DATE: ___/___/___

SPEAKER: _____

SERMON: _____ BOOK OF: _____

SERMON NOTES:
_____
_____
_____
_____
_____
_____
_____
_____

PERSONAL REFLECTIONS:
_____
_____
_____
_____
_____
_____
_____
_____
_____

Prayer Journal

TITLE: _____ DATE: ___/___/____

SPEAKER: _____

SERMON: _____ BOOK OF: _____

SERMON NOTES:

_____
_____
_____
_____
_____
_____
_____

PERSONAL REFLECTIONS:

_____
_____
_____
_____
_____
_____
_____
_____
_____
_____

Prayer Journal

TITLE: _____ DATE: ___/___/___

SPEAKER: _____

SERMON: _____ BOOK OF: _____

SERMON NOTES:
_____
_____
_____
_____
_____
_____
_____
_____

PERSONAL REFLECTIONS:
_____
_____
_____
_____
_____
_____
_____
_____
_____
_____

Prayer Journal

TITLE: _____ DATE: ___/___/___

SPEAKER: _____

SERMON: _____ BOOK OF: _____

SERMON NOTES:

_____
_____
_____
_____
_____
_____
_____

PERSONAL REFLECTIONS:

_____
_____
_____
_____
_____
_____
_____
_____
_____

Prayer Journal

TITLE: _____ DATE: ___/___/____

SPEAKER: _____

SERMON: _____ BOOK OF: _____

SERMON NOTES:
_____
_____
_____
_____
_____
_____
_____
_____

PERSONAL REFLECTIONS:
_____
_____
_____
_____
_____
_____
_____
_____
_____
_____

Prophetic Dreams & Notes

Notes

Notes

Notes

Notes

Notes

Notes

Notes

Notes

Notes

Notes

Notes

Notes

Notes

Notes

Notes

Notes

Notes

Notes

Notes

Notes

IMANI M-GLOVER

About the Author

Imani M-Glover is a California native who resides in the Bay Area with her husband, two sons, and a bonus baby. She is the author of two books, the first being a collaborative work titled, "Before the Vows Break " which shares tales of triumph and gives advice to wives and wives to be. Her second piece of literature "Glorifying Grace Journal" is a faith based Journal which helps readers in their walk of faith by recording prayer requests and giving believers a place to document their faithfulness of the Lord.

Imani is also the owner of The Lemonade Bar located in Oakland California. The next time you are in The Bay area look her up and have a refreshing drink!

Contact Imani
Email: imanimglover@yahoo.com
Website: www.imanimglover.com.

www.ingramcontent.com/pod-product-compliance
Lightning Source LLC
Chambersburg PA
CBHW031149160426
43193CB00008B/305